AF334895

Letter of the

New Canadian Poets

Master of Horse

Gary Geddes

Oberon Press

This poem was awarded the E. J. Pratt
medal and prize for poetry in 1969 at
the University of Toronto. An earlier
version was broadcast on CBC radio's
Anthology and printed, in part, in the
author's first collection, POEM.

For Hugo and Louise McPherson

I was signed
on the King's authority
as master of horse.
Three days
              (I remember
              quite clearly)
three days after we parted.
I did not really believe it
it seemed so much the unrolling
of an incredible dream.

Bright plumes, scarlet tunics,
glint of sunlight on armour.
Fifty of the King's best horses,
strong, high-spirited, rearing
to the blast of trumpets,
galloping
down the long avenida
to the waiting ships.
And me, your gangling brother,
permitted to ride with cavalry.

Laughter,
children singing
in the market, women
dancing, throwing flowers,
the whole street covered
with flowers.

In the plaza del sol
a blind beggar kissed my eyes.
I hadn't expected the softness
of his fingers
                moving upon my face.

A bad beginning.
The animals knew, hesitated
at the ramps, backed off,
finally had to be blindfolded
and beaten aboard.

The sailors grumbled for days
as if we had brought on board
a cargo of women.

But the sea smiled.
It smiled as we passed
through the world's gate,
smiled as we lost our escort
of gulls. I have seen
such smiles on faces of whores
in Barcelona.

For months now
an unwelcome guest
in my own body.
I squat by the fire
in a silence broken only
by the tireless grinding
of insects.

I have taken
to drawing your face
in the brown earth
at my feet.
         (The ears are
         never quite right.)

Perhaps Father Antonio would
let me paint the angels
for fiesta. You laugh?
It is a sound unheard
in this place, where
one needs angels more
than bread.

You are waving,
waving.
Your tears are a river
that swells, rushes beside me.
I lie for days in a sea drier
than the desert of the Moors,
but your tears are lost,
sucked
into the parched throat of the sky.

I am watched daily.
The ship's carpenter is at work
nearby, within the stockade,
fashioning a harness for me,
a wooden collar. He is a fool
who takes no pride in his work,
yet the chips lie about his feet,
beautiful as yellow petals.

Days melt
in the hot sun, flow
together. An order is given
to jettison the horses,
it sweeps like a breeze
over parched black faces.

I am not consulted, though
Ortega comes to me later
when it is over and says:

    God knows, there are men
    I'd have worried less to lose.

The sailors are relieved,
fall to it with abandon.
The first horse is blindfolded,
led to the gunwales, and struck
so hard it leaps skyward
in an arc, its great body
silhouetted against the sun.

I remember thinking
how graceless it looked,
out of its element, legs
braced and stiffened
for the plunge.

They drink long
draughts, muzzles submerged
to the eyes, set out like spokes
in all directions.
The salt does its work.
The first scream, proud head
thrown back, nostrils flared,
flesh tight over teeth
and gums
              (yellow teeth,
              bloody gums).
The spasms, heaving bodies,
turning, turning.
I am the centre
of this churning circumference.
The wretch beside me,
fingers
knotted to the gunwales.

They plunge toward
the ship, hooves crashing
on the planked hull.
Soft muzzles, ripped
and bleeding on splintered
wood and barnacles.
The ensign's mare
struggles half out of the water
on the backs of two
hapless animals.

When the affair ended
the sea was littered with bodies,
smooth bloated carcasses.
Neither pike-pole nor ship's
boats could keep them off.
Sailors that never missed
a meal retched violently
in the hot sun. Only
the silent industry of sharks
could give them rest.

What is the shape of freedom
after all? Did I come here
to be devoured by insects, or
maddened by screams in the night?

Ortega, when we found him,
pinned and swinging in his bones,
jawbone pinned and singing
in the wind, God's lieutenant,
more eloquent in death.

Sooner or later all hope
evaporates, joy itself
is seasonal. The others?
They are Spaniards, no more
no less, and burn with a lust
that sends them tilting
at the sun itself.

Ortega, listen, the horses,
where are the sun's horses
to pull his chariot from the sea,
end this conspiracy of dark?

The nights are long, the cold
a maggot boarding in my flesh.

I hear them moving,
barely perceptible at first,
faint as the roar of insects,
gathering
gathering to thunder
across the hidden valleys
of the sea, crash of hooves
upon my door, hot quick
breath upon my face.

My eyes, he kissed my eyes,
the softness of his fingers
moving. . . .

Forgive me, I did not
mean this to be my final offering.
Sometimes the need
to forgive, be forgiven,
makes the heart a pilgrim.
I am no traveller.
My Christopher was faceless
with rubbing on the voyage out,
the voyage into exile.
Islanded in our separate
selves, words are
too frail a bridge.

I see you in the morning
running to meet me down
the mountainside, your face
transfigured with happiness.
Wait for me, my sister,
where wind rubs bare
the cliff-face, where we rode
to watch the passing ships
at daybreak, and saw them
burn golden, from masthead
down to waterline.

I will come soon

Library of Congress
Catalogue Card No. 73-76039

ISBN   0 88750 073 0 (hardcover)
ISBN   0 88750 074 9 (softcover)

Designed and printed in Canada
at The Coach House Press, Toronto

Published in Canada by Oberon Press